How Do I Use a Thesaurus?

Susan Meyer

IN ASSOCIATION WITH

EDUCATIONAL SERVICES

Published in 2015 by Britannica Educational Publishing (a trademark of Encyclopædia Britannica, Inc.) in association with The Rosen Publishing Group, Inc.
29 East 21st Street, New York, NY 10010

Distributed exclusively by Rosen Publishing.
To see additional Britannica Educational Publishing titles, go to rosenpublishing.com.

First Edition

Britannica Educational Publishing
J.E. Luebering: Director, Core Reference Group
Mary Rose McCudden: Editor, Britannica Student Encyclopedia

Rosen Publishing
Hope Lourie Killcoyne: Executive Editor
John Murphy: Editor
Nelson Sá: Art Director
Brian Garvey: Designer
Cindy Reiman: Photography Manager
Marty Levick: Photo Researcher

Cataloging-in-Publication Data

Meyer, Susan, 1986-
How do I use a thesaurus?/Susan Meyer.—First Edition.
        pages cm.—(Research tools you can use)
Includes bibliographical references and index.
Audience: Grades 3-6.
ISBN 978-1-62275-369-7 (library bound)—ISBN 978-1-62275-371-0 (pbk.)—
ISBN 978-1-62275-372-7 (6-pack)
1. English language—Synonyms and antonyms—Dictionaries, Juvenile. 2. English language—Synonyms and antonyms—Juvenile literature. I. Title.
PE1591.M49 2014
423'.12028—dc23
                                                            2014002136

Manufactured in the United States of America

Photo credits:
Cover and interior pages (background) © iStockphoto.com/Acerebel; cover (inset from left) violetblue/Shutterstock .com, Jupiterimages/Stockbyte/Thinkstock, Viorika Prikhodko/E+/Getty Images; pp. 4–5 Peter Fuchs/Shutterstock .com; p. 6 Fuse/Thinkstock; p. 7 Pressmaster/Shutterstock.com; p. 9 Hulton Archive/Getty Images; pp. 10–11 Ron Chapple Studios/Hemera/Thinkstock; p. 13 Arena Photo UK/Shutterstock.com; p. 16 © iStockphoto.com/Miquel Munill; p. 18 michaeljung/Shutterstock.com; p. 19 Dan Kosmayer/Shutterstock.com; p. 21 Sabphoto/Shutterstock .com; p. 23 Elena Elisseeva/Shutterstock.com; p. 24 Jani Bryson/iStock/Thinkstock; p. 26 Dmitry Kalinovsky/Shutter stock.com; p. 27 Ingram Publishing/Thinkstock; p. 28 kali9/E+/Getty Images.

CONTENTS

CHAPTER 1

What Is a Thesaurus?

A thesaurus is a reference work that groups words together by similar meanings. If you wanted to find another word for "happy," a thesaurus might point you to the word "cheerful." Thesauri (the word for more than one thesaurus) help people to communicate.

WHY DO I NEED A THESAURUS?

Everyone loves a well-told story. Great stories have interesting characters. Readers can picture what the characters look like and what they do. Great stories make readers laugh or cry.

What Is a Thesaurus?

A thesaurus might help you to describe the boy in the picture as "joyous," "triumphant," or even "jubilant."

They make readers turn the page quickly to find out what happens next! All of that is achieved with words. Choosing the right words will make your writing stand out. That means it will be entertaining for readers.

The word thesaurus comes from Latin, a language that was spoken in ancient Rome. It means "treasure store" or a place to keep something valuable. Are words really valuable? Think of how it feels when you don't understand something. Now think about how it feels when someone explains it in words you can understand!

How Do I Use a Thesaurus?

A talented writer who uses exciting words can make a reader get caught up in a story.

Writing a good story can be fun. But it can also be hard work. Fortunately, writers have tools they can use to help them. A thesaurus is a tool that will help you find just the right word. This will make your stories interesting. If you want readers to laugh or cry with your

WHAT IS A THESAURUS?

Using a thesaurus is easy and can be fun once you understand how it is organized.

characters, and if you want them to keep turning the page, then you might find a thesaurus helpful.

WHAT DOES A THESAURUS DO?

Every language has thousands of different words. Words have meanings, called definitions. To look up the definition of a word, you need a dictionary. To find words with similar meanings, you use a thesaurus. Words with similar meanings are synonyms. Some synonyms for "cold" are "icy" or "freezing." A thesaurus can give you even more impressive synonyms, like "biting" or "arctic."

A thesaurus has another function. It gives you opposite meanings for words. A word that is opposite in meaning to another word is an

PETER MARK ROGET

Peter Mark Roget was born in England in 1779. He studied medicine and became a doctor. However, Roget was also fascinated by words. He gathered a list of words and organized them by their meanings. In 1852, his book of words was published. It was one of the first modern thesauri. Roget's first thesaurus had 15,000 words in it. Today, the book we now call *Roget's Thesaurus* has more than 260,000 synonyms. Roget died in 1869 at the age of 90.

antonym. For example, "dry" is an antonym of "wet."

Roget's Thesaurus is one of the best-known thesauri. You might have one right now in your class-room. Like diction-aries, thesauri have been around for a long time because they provide useful information.

CHAPTER 2

How to Use a Thesaurus

A thesaurus is a valuable **reference** source. It helps you use and understand words with similar meanings. If "good" was the only word to describe something that wasn't bad, writing would be very boring. Using synonyms can make your writing more exciting. Whether you are writing a book report for school, a letter to a friend, or a story just for fun, all writing can be improved with well-chosen words.

A thesaurus is just one of many reference books that can help you find information.

WHAT KIND OF THESAURUS SHOULD I USE?

Ask your teacher or school librarian to help you find a thesaurus. You can also buy one of your own. Once you have a thesaurus, you have to know how to use it. Luckily, most thesauri are easy to use and understand. The first step when opening a new thesaurus is

A reference book contains specific information. For example, an atlas is a book of maps. You would use it to find out where a place is. It has information like names of capital cities or towns. A guidebook gives more detailed information. A traveler could use it to find out what to do in a particular place. Atlases, guidebooks, dictionaries, and thesauri are all examples of reference books.

II

to figure out what type it is. There are two main types of thesaurus. One is an A-to-Z thesaurus, and the other is an index thesaurus or Roget-style thesaurus. Read the introduction to find out which kind of thesaurus you have.

A-to-Z thesauri are simpler to use. Their words are arranged alphabetically, like the dictionary. If you are looking for the word "good," you would search under "G." Next to the entry for the word "good" will be a list of synonyms and antonyms.

In an index thesaurus or Roget-style thesaurus, the words are arranged by meaning. To locate the word "good" in this type of thesaurus, look at the index. The index is an alphabetical list

This is an example of an A-to-Z thesaurus, where entries are listed alphabetically.

of words. So "good" will be with the other "G" words. Next to the word, you will find a list of page numbers. These page numbers show where "good" is listed as a synonym or antonym.

A word entry in a thesaurus will almost always include the same basic information. It will list the word. It will also sometimes give a short definition for the word. Under that, it will list the word's part of speech. Some words can have more than one part of speech. For example, the word "walk" can be a verb ("walk the dog") or a noun ("go for a walk"). This word would have two entries in a thesaurus. After each part of speech, the entry will include a list of synonyms for the word. Below will be the list of antonyms. You can choose the word from the list that best fits what you are writing.

CHAPTER 3

Computer and Online Thesauri

You don't have to use a book to find synonyms and antonyms. If you have access to a computer, you may be able to use a feature in a program or an online tool. Both are easy to use.

A THESAURUS IN YOUR COMPUTER

Most **word processing** programs have a thesaurus feature. This allows writers to find just the right word with the click of an icon.

Most word-processing programs have a toolbar.

A **word processor** is any computer program that is used for storing, creating, or formatting text. Word processors are found on almost all computers. They provide helpful tools like spelling and grammar check, a dictionary, a thesaurus, and word counting.

This is a list of icons, or images. Clicking on them will do things like underline, boldface, or change the size of the text. Look for an icon or label for reviewing or editing your writing.

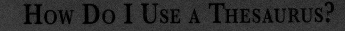

Built-in thesauri in word-processing programs make writing and editing easier.

The thesaurus icon or label will most likely be near the "Spelling" or "Spell Check" tool. Another way is to highlight the word you want to replace with a synonym or antonym using your mouse or track pad. When you click on the word, a box will appear and one of the options will be "Synonyms." Moving your mouse over that option will give you a list of possible replacements for the word.

A THESAURUS ON THE WEB

To use an online thesaurus, you first need a computer with Internet access. If you do not have one at home, you can find one at the public library or in your school library or computer lab. An online thesaurus can be used in any web browser. A good online thesaurus can be found at www.merriam-webster.com.

With an online thesaurus you can locate synonyms and antonyms without even turning a

Whether writing an essay for school or a story for fun, online thesauri can be a big help in finding just the right words.

page. You simply type the word for which you would like to find a synonym or antonym in the search box. When you enter the word, the online thesaurus quickly shows all related entries. The first entry will be for the word you entered. Under that, you will see all of the entries where the word you searched appears as one of the synonyms or antonyms. Using an online thesaurus can be like getting the best of both worlds between an A-to-Z thesaurus and an index-style thesaurus. Plus, no paper cuts!

CHAPTER 4

Tips for Using a Thesaurus

Once you get the hang of using a thesaurus, you can use it anytime. A thesaurus will help you make your writing stronger. But there are some tips that you should follow.

DON'T BE BORING!

A well-chosen word can make your writing stronger and more interesting. You should not repeat the same word over and over again. This is called repetition. Repetition is boring for a reader. The more you write, the more you may find repetition boring as a writer, too. But don't overuse your thesaurus! Changing just

Careful use of a thesaurus helps liven up your writing for both you and the reader.

a few words may make your writing stronger. That does not mean that changing more words will make your writing super strong. In fact, if you change too many words, your writing can become awkward. You want your writing to sound like you wrote it. So keep some words that you would normally use.

Another thing to remember is that bigger words are not always better. Choose a word that best fits the sentence, not just the word that sounds the smartest.

WHAT'S THE RIGHT WORD?

Synonyms are words that have *similar* meanings. They are not exactly the same. Synonyms can have slightly different definitions. Never just swap a word for a synonym and think it will be a perfect fit. The meaning of any word you use has to be just right. If you don't know the exact meaning of a word, look it up. It is a good idea to have a dictionary around as well as a thesaurus. It can tell you if the word you chose is a good match for your sentence.

Also think about the feeling that people have about a word. This is called a word's **connotation**. Think of the words "youthful" and "childish." They mean almost the same thing. But

Does the word "youthful" or "childish" describe the girl in this picture?

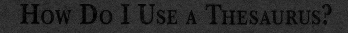

A word's connotation is all of the different thoughts and feelings that people have about that word. Words and language are constantly changing and evolving as people's feelings change. Some words even change their meanings over time. For example, the word "cool" is a synonym for "great." But long ago, the meaning of "cool" dealt only with temperature.

you may have different feelings about each word. Would you rather be called one over the other? When choosing a replacement, a thesaurus can only do part of the work for you. You also have to make careful choices.

CHAPTER 5

Making Writing Pop

Now you know how to use a thesaurus and thoughtfully choose synonym replacements. This will make your writing pop. It is now time to try it out for yourself.

FIND THE RIGHT WORD

Read the following story:

Doug is a <u>nice</u> dog. He lives with a <u>good</u> family. One day, Doug <u>walks</u> to the park. The weather is <u>bad</u> that day. Doug loses his way. He is <u>scared</u>. Suddenly, he sees a <u>house</u>. Could it be his? He sees his family waving from the front porch. "Come inside where it's warm, Doug!" Doug is <u>happy</u> to be home.

The story is pretty dull. Part of the problem is that the words are so plain. Using a thesaurus, you can make the writing stronger. On paper or a computer, rewrite the story. Replace some of the underlined words with synonyms. Pay attention to the part of speech of the word you are replacing. Is it a noun, a verb, or an adjective? The replacement word

Carefully choose which words you want to replace. Changing all of them could make your writing awkward.

should be the same part of speech as the original word. Use a classroom thesaurus, the thesaurus in your computer program, or an online thesaurus.

COMPARE WITH PEERS

Share your story with classmates who have also rewritten this story. Notice

With a thesaurus, the knowledge of how to use it, and a willingness to edit, you are well on your way to becoming an excellent writer!

By sharing your work, you can get feedback from other students on your writing. Your peers might even have ideas that will improve your story.

how different each person's story is now. The meaning of the story can change just by changing a few words. For example, look at the word "house." If this word was changed to "shack," it would paint a completely different picture than if it had been changed to the word "mansion." This is why synonyms are part of the foundation of **creative writing.**

Now you have had some practice using a thesaurus. You can use this tool to make all of your writing stronger!

Creative writing expresses ideas and feelings. It does not just give information. It is usually a story, like a play, novel, or poem. Creative writing can be fiction or nonfiction. An autobiography is a story that someone tells with facts about his or her own life. This is an example of creative writing. A short story about a made-up character is also an example of creative writing.

alphabetically Arranged in the order of the letters of the alphabet.

antonym A word of opposite meaning.

communicate To give information by speaking or writing.

definition The meaning of a word or word group.

entries Items noted as a headword with a definition or identification.

language A system of words used to express thoughts and feelings.

part of speech A class of words (such as adjectives, nouns, or verbs) identified according to the kinds of ideas they express and the way they work in a sentence.

publish To prepare or produce written work for distribution to others.

replacements Items that take the place of others.

synonym A word having the same or almost the same meaning as another word.

web browser A program used to view content on the Internet.

BOOKS

Cleary, Brian P., and Brian Gable. *Stroll and Walk, Babble and Talk: More About Synonyms*. New York, NY: Millbrook Press, 2010.

Hellweg, Paul. *The American Heritage Children's Thesaurus*. Boston, MA: American Heritage, 2012.

Matchett, Carol. *First Dictionary and Thesaurus Activities*. Huddersfield, England: Schofield and Sims, 2009.

Wilcox, Alison. *Descriptosaurus: Supporting Creative Writing*. New York, NY: Routledge, 2013.

WEBSITES

Because of the changing nature of Internet links, Rosen Publishing has developed an online list of websites related to the subject of this book. This site is updated regularly. Please use this link to access the list:

http://www.rosenlinks.com/RTYCU/Thes

INDEX